CHANGING WORLD
IRAQ

CHANGING WORLD

IRAQ

Geoff Barker

ARCTURUS

This edition first published by Arcturus Publishing
Distributed by Black Rabbit Books
P.O. Box 3263
Mankato
Minnesota MN 56002

Copyright © 2008 Arcturus Publishing Limited

Printed in the United States

Library of Congress Cataloging-in-Publication Data

Barker, Geoff, 1963-
  Iraq / Geoff Barker.
      p. cm. -- (Changing world)
  ISBN 978-1-84837-008-1
  1. Iraq--Juvenile literature. I. Title.

  DS70.62.K66 2009
  956.7--dc22

                              2008016658

Series concept: Alex Woolf
Editor: Alex Woolf
Designer: Ian Winton
Illustrator: Stefan Chabluk
Picture researcher: Alex Woolf

Picture credits:
Art Archive: 12 (Turkish and Islamic Art Museum, Istanbul/Alfredo Dagli Orti).
Corbis: cover left (Peter Turnley), cover right (Ali Abbas/epa), 6 (Nik Wheeler), 7 (Ed Kashi), 10 (Bettmann), 11 (Abilio Lope), 14 (Slhaldeen Rasheed/Reuters), 15 (In Visu/Corbis), 16 (Patrick Robert/Sygma), 17 (Ali Abbas/epa), 19 (Thaier al-Sudani/Reuters), 20 (Michael S Yamashita), 22 (Ceerwan Aziz/Reuters), 23 (Cheryl Diaz Meyer/Dallas Morning News), 24 (Stephanie Sinclair), 26 (Iraqi Prime Minister Office/Handout/epa), 27 (Ceerwan Aziz/Pool/epa), 28 (Thaier al-Sudani/Reuters), 31 (Ali Haider/epa), 32 (Faleh Kheiber/Reuters), 35 (Ali Abbas/epa), 39 (Aladin Abdel Naby/Reuters), 40 (Youssef Badawi/epa), 43 (Patrick Robert).
Getty Images: 13 (AFP), 25 (AFP), 36, 37 (AFP), 38, 41 (AFP).

The illustrations on pages 8, 9, 18, 30, and 33 are by Stefan Chabluk.

Cover captions
Left: On April 10, 2003, the day after US troops entered the center of Baghdad, a crowd toppled a statue of Saddam Hussein near the Palestine Hotel.
Right: Iraqi pupils sit in their classroom at one of Baghdad's elementary schools on the second day of the new school year, September 13, 2005.

Contents

CHAPTER 1

★ Introduction

Iraq lies at the very heart of the Middle East, like a triangular-shaped wedge between the countries of Saudi Arabia, Syria, and Iran. It also shares much shorter borders with Kuwait to the southeast, Jordan to the west, and Turkey in the north. Today's Iraq was once known as the ancient land of Mesopotamia, or land "between the rivers," of the Tigris and Euphrates. The land's fertile soils made it a natural site for some of the world's earliest civilizations—Sumerians,

PHYSICAL GEOGRAPHY

Area:
  total: 170,458 sq mi (437,072 sq km)
  land: 168,543 sq mi (432,162 sq km)
  water: 1,915 sq mi (4,910 sq km)
Highest point: unnamed peak—11,844 ft (3,611 m)
(local Kurdish name: Cheekha Dar, or "black tent")
Lowest point: Persian Gulf—0 ft (0 m)
Land boundaries:
  total: 2,263 mi (3,650 km)
  border countries: Iran 904 mi (1,458 km), Jordan 112 mi (181 km), Kuwait 149 mi (240 km), Saudi Arabia 505 mi (814 km), Syria 375 mi (605 km), Turkey 218 mi (352 km)
Coastline: 36 mi (58 km)

Source: *CIA World Factbook*

Akkadians, Babylonians, and Assyrians. Underneath its soil lies Iraq's richest resource: oil. Iraq now has the world's third-largest proven conventional crude oil reserves.

Lowlands, deserts, and mountains

Situated in central and southeastern Iraq, the broad floodplains of the Tigris-Euphrates basin

Many ancient cities grew up along the banks of the Euphrates River. At nearly 1,736 mi (2,800 km) long, the river runs from Turkey to the Persian Gulf. Much of its central section, like here in Khan al-Baghdadi in the province of al-Anbar, is lined with date palm groves.

The Zagros Mountains, in the northeastern region of Iraq, form a natural geographic barrier between Iraq's central plains and the Iranian plateau to the east. Mostly situated in Iran, the Zagros range is about 558 mi (900 km) long and 2149 mi (40 km) wide.

make up about a third of the country. Much of this land has rich soil that was once ideal for agriculture. However, it has been over-irrigated, and some of it has been abandoned owing to its high salt content. Although lowlands form much of the landscape of Iraq, highlands rise to the north and northeast, including the high elevations of the Kurdistan region. The Anti-Taurus and Zagros mountains form the borders with Turkey and Iran respectively. Between Iraq's two great rivers in the north is an arid plateau in an upland region known as al-Jazirah, or "the island." Here, the Sinjar Mountains rise to a height of over 4,920 ft (1,500 m). Forty percent of Iraq's land area

consists of vast deserts in the west and south, including the western desert region, called Wadiyah, which is almost 1,640 ft (500 m) above sea level.

Two rivers

Iraq's two mighty rivers, the Tigris and the Euphrates, begin their journey farther north in Turkey and flow in a southeasterly direction along roughly parallel courses through the country until they meet at the southern Iraqi town of al-Qurnah. The merged river, called the Shatt al-Arab, or "stream of the Arabs," continues south for the final 124 mi (200 km) of its route to the coast. The Shatt al-Arab passes the port of Basra, where it forms part of the eastern boundary with Iran, before finally emptying into the Persian Gulf. With Kuwait to the west and Iran to the east, Iraq's coastline on the Persian Gulf is a short stretch of only 36 mi (58 km).

This chart shows the climate of Baghdad. Situated in Iraq's central plains, the city has average daily temperatures of nearly 95°F (35°C) in July and August. Temperatures as high as 124°F (51°C) have been recorded in the summer.

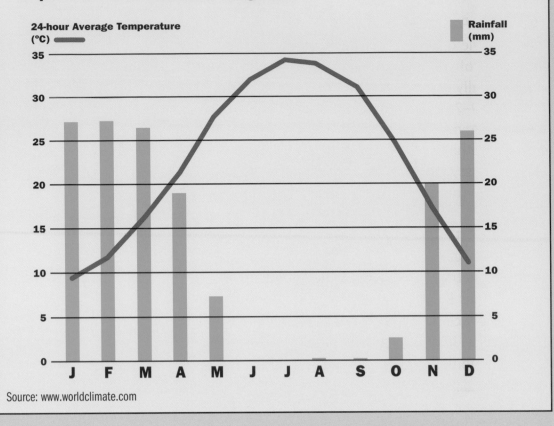

Temperature and rainfall in Baghdad

24-hour Average Temperature (°C)

Rainfall (mm)

Source: www.worldclimate.com

Climate

Most of Iraq, including the lowlands, experiences long, hot, dry summers lasting from May to October, although the weather can be more humid near the rivers. Winters are short and mild, with almost all rain falling between November and April. Desert regions have blisteringly hot, dry summers, while the damper northeast of the country has shorter, cooler summers. Precipitation in the northeastern highlands can be in excess of 39 inches (1,000 mm) during the year, much of which falls during the winter as snow. Heavy snows melting in spring can cause flooding farther south in central and southern Iraq.

Culture

Iraq has a rich history of ancient civilizations stretching back over 7,000 years. Today, 97 percent of Iraq's approximately 27 million people are Muslim. The Sunni faith is dominant in the surrounding Arab countries, such as Saudi Arabia, Kuwait, and Jordan, but Shia Muslims form the majority in Iraq, outnumbering Sunni Muslims by roughly two to one. Despite religious and political differences, Shia and Sunni Muslims are ethnically similar. Both Shia and Sunni Muslims place great importance on their immediate family as well as more tribal links with their extended family.

The country's major languages are Arabic and Kurdish. About 25 million Kurds live in a mountainous region running across Syria, Turkey, Iran, and Iraq. Most of Iraq's 6 million Kurds speak a dialect called Kurdi, or Sorani, which is the official form of Kurdish and similar to the modern Persian language of Farsi. Most Kurds are Sunni Muslims. They have retained their own distinctive cultural identity, notably their music and dance.

The Marsh Arabs live in southern Iraq. Although their lifestyle has remained largely unchanged for thousands of years, the Marsh Arabs' culture was almost totally destroyed under Saddam Hussein (ruled 1979–2003). A tiny number of Marsh Arabs still survive, making reed boats and fishing. Iraq has many other small ethnic groups, including Christian Assyrians, the seminomadic Muslim Turkmen of the north, Turks, and Armenians.

Urban centers

Urban life began in the Middle East thousands of years ago as traders exchanged their goods in cities such as Babylon, built in about 2000 BCE in what is now central Iraq. Although Babylon no longer exists, Iraq has many large cities and towns, which are home to 70 percent of the population.

- Baghdad, on the Tigris River in central Iraq, was founded in 762 CE by the caliph Mansur. Baghdad is the capital of Iraq, with a population of nearly 6 million.
- Mosul is situated on the banks of the Tigris in northern Iraq. Its population of around 2 million is mainly Kurdish, with a large minority of Christian Arabs.
- Basra, in southeastern Iraq, is the country's major port. Basra is a center of oil refining, and its location on the Shatt al-Arab waterway is ideal for exporting oil.

Iraq shares its borders with six other countries. Jordan and Syria are to the west, with Saudi Arabia to the south, Turkey to the north, and Kuwait to the southeast. Its longest boundary—904 mi (1,458 km)—is with Iran, to the east.

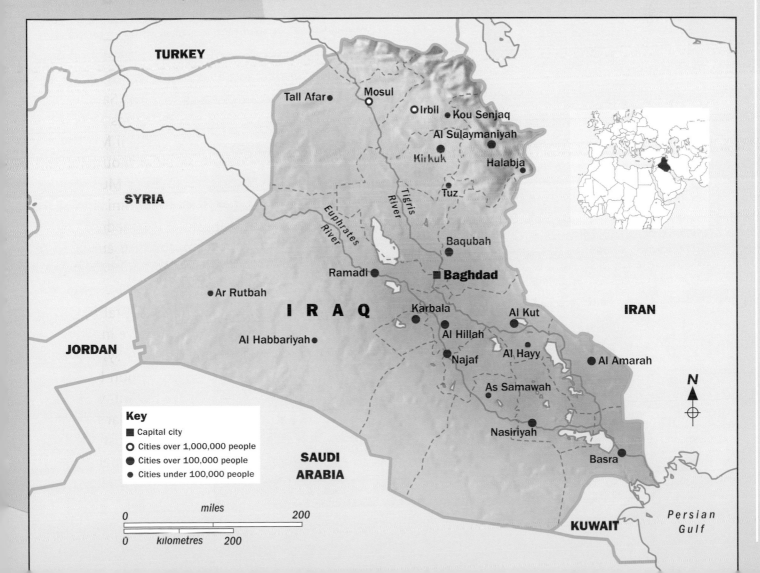

Key
- ■ Capital city
- ○ Cities over 1,000,000 people
- ● Cities over 100,000 people
- • Cities under 100,000 people

CHAPTER 2

★ History

The very first human settlements, or societies, began to grow in an area called the "fertile crescent," curving around from the Nile River valley of ancient Egypt into Mesopotamia, or today's Iraq. Eight thousand years ago, small settlements developed in the upper valley of the Tigris and Euphrates rivers. Instead of moving on, nomads started to settle down and irrigate the plains with ditches for agriculture.

Early history

The most notable of Mesopotamia's early settlers were the Sumerians, whom experts generally credit with inventing cuneiform, the first form of writing. The Sumerians wrote down the earliest surviving epic poems and invented the plow and probably the wheel, too.

Babylon

The famous ancient city of Babylon was established in modern-day Iraq, nearly 62 mi (100 km) south of Baghdad. In the 1700s BCE, a great warrior named Hammurabi took power in the region and founded the Babylonian empire. Adopting the Sumerian form of writing, King Hammurabi wrote down one of the earliest written collections of laws, known as the Code of Hammurabi. Babylon's golden era occurred in the first half of the sixth century BCE, during the rule of King Nebuchadnezzar II. He built the Hanging Gardens of Babylon,

The Hanging Gardens of Babylon were one of the Seven Wonders of the Ancient World. There is still controversy about their location, but most experts believe they were in or near the royal palace in Babylon.

Samarra, on the Tigris River in central Iraq, is one of the largest archaeological sites in the world. The ninth-century Great Mosque and the famous al-Malwiyah, a spiral minaret, are remarkable monuments of the Abbasid caliphate. Samarra is a center of pilgrimage for Shia Muslims.

one of the Seven Wonders of the Ancient World. Today, very little remains of Nebuchadnezzar's Summer Palace, which is thought to have once contained the Hanging Gardens.

Foreign domination

From the sixth century BCE, the lands of Mesopotamia were conquered by a succession of different empire builders. Persia (today's Iran) invaded the country in 539 BCE. Then in 331 BCE, Greece, under Alexander the Great, defeated the Persians. Two hundred years later, the Persians once again ruled Babylon.

A new era in Iraq's history began in 637 CE, with the arrival of Arab armies from the Arabian Peninsula, south of Mesopotamia. The Muslim Arabs defeated the Persian rulers of Mesopotamia

at Qadisiyah on the Euphrates. Baghdad was founded in the middle of the eighth century. The city and its surrounding region were ruled by the caliph, or leader, al-Mansur, from the Abbasid dynasty. For the next 500 years, Abbasid caliphs ruled Mesopotamia. Under their rule, Baghdad became one of the world's most beautiful cities and a great center of learning and Arabic culture. Al-Kufa (105 mi, or 170 km, south of Baghdad) and Mosul (in northern Iraq) were also important Arab cities.

FOCUS: DIVISION AMONG MUSLIMS

The Muslim faith was founded by the prophet Mohammed (c. 570–632 CE). After his death, there was a dispute over the leadership of Islam. One group believed that the caliph should come from Mohammed's own family. Ali, Mohammed's son-in-law and cousin, thought he should be caliph, and his group became known as the Shi'at Ali (faction, or party, of Ali), now called the Shias. Although Ali was recognized in Mesopotamia and Persia, a second and larger group, centered on Damascus in Syria, followed a different successor, Mu'awiya ibn Abi Sufyan. These Sunni Muslims believed that the best spiritual leader should be chosen and that he did not necessarily need to descend directly from the Prophet.

Ottoman Empire

From the 13th century, Mesopotamia fell to a series of conquerors. In 1258, the Mongol chief Hulagu invaded Iraq and captured Baghdad, killing the last Abbasid caliph. The city was conquered again in 1405 by Tamerlane, a warlord of Turco-Mongol descent. Finally, in 1534, Baghdad was taken by the Ottoman Turks. The Ottoman state was founded by Osman I in the 14th century. Like the Mongols, the Ottoman Turks were great cavalrymen, and by the middle of the 17th century, they had built an empire that dominated the Middle East and southeastern Europe. In the 19th century, the Ottoman Turks finally conquered the whole region of Mesopotamia, which they divided into the three provinces of Mosul, Baghdad, and Basra.

Mesopotamia remained part of the Ottoman Empire until the 20th century, by which time the empire was in severe decline. During World War I (1914–18), the Turkish Ottoman Empire allied itself with Germany and Austria-Hungary against the United Kingdom (UK), France, and Russia. Britain encouraged the Arabs in Mesopotamia to fight against the Ottoman Turks, promising them independence after the war. Instead, the victorious powers divided up the Ottoman empire and the British were given a mandate to rule Mesopotamia, which became the new state of Iraq.

Independence

In 1921, the British installed Faisal I as emir (king) of Iraq to give their mandate legitimacy. He was a member of the Hashemites, an important Arab dynasty, and had been a key ally of the British during World War I. Under Faisal, a political elite of rich Sunni Muslims wielded

Murat IV, sultan of the Ottoman Empire from 1623 to 1640, was a feared warrior who recaptured Baghdad in 1638, following its loss to the Persians in 1623.

considerable influence. In 1927, significant quantities of oil were discovered. Iraq officially gained its independence in 1932, but Britain retained significant political power in the country, determined to keep control of Iraqi oil.

The monarchy lasted until July 14, 1958, when it was overthrown in a bloody military coup by an army officer, General Abdel Karim Kassem, who established the Republic of Iraq. Another coup in 1963 ended Kassem's rule. Then, in 1968, a bloodless coup by the Baath (meaning Renaissance) Party put General Ahmad Hassan al-Bakr in power.

CASE STUDY: SHATT AL-ARAB DISPUTE

The strategically important Shatt al-Arab waterway, with its outlet in the Persian Gulf, had been a source of dispute between the Ottoman and Persian empires since a roughly drawn-up peace treaty in the 17th century. In 1975, Iraq and Iran signed the Algiers Accord, which recognized midstream as the border between the two countries. Saddam Hussein tried to revoke this agreement in 1980, prior to invading Iran. He claimed the whole waterway, up to the Iranian shore, for Iraq.

Reign of Saddam Hussein

In January 1969, Saddam Hussein became vice president of the Baath Party, but as President al-Bakr's health worsened, Saddam assumed greater control. During the 1970s, Saddam became the effective ruler of the country, using the political police to remove unwanted opponents or politicians. In 1979, he formally assumed the presidency of Iraq, and his reign of terror gained momentum. That year, he executed a quarter of

the Revolutionary Command Council (RCC), the body of senior officials that helped to govern Iraq.

Saddam was concerned by developments in neighboring Iran. In February 1979, the Shia cleric Ayatollah Khomeini inspired the Islamic Revolution. Saddam Hussein and his secular (nonreligious), Sunni-dominated government feared that Iraqi Shias (who formed the majority in Iraq) might be encouraged to attempt a Shia revolution in their own country. There were other sources of tension between Iraq and Iran, including a long-standing dispute over the boundary of the Shatt al-Arab waterway, which Iran and Iraq shared. Saddam also wished to annex the southern provinces of Iran, where many of Iran's oil fields were concentrated.

Vice President Saddam Hussein (left) is pictured here in 1976 with President al-Bakr. Al-Bakr resigned in July 1979, when Saddam formally took over power. Saddam's brutal reign was to last over 20 years.

The Iran-Iraq War

On September 22, 1980, Iraq launched an offensive across the Shatt al-Arab into Iran. The war lasted eight years and claimed over a million military and civilian lives. During the war, Iraq received support from Western governments as well as other Arab governments who feared the spread of Iran's Islamic Revolution. Saddam Hussein called an end to the war in August 1988. He had accomplished little through the conflict, despite the terrible cost. The border between the two countries remained unchanged.

Invasion of Kuwait

Arab countries, including neighboring Kuwait, had helped to fund Iraq's costly and destructive war with Iran, and by 1988, Iraq was heavily in debt to them. On August 2, 1990, Saddam invaded oil-rich Kuwait as an answer to his country's deepening economic problems,

CASE STUDY: HALABJA

Before the end of the Iran-Iraq war, in March 1988, Saddam turned his attention to the Kurds in northern Iraq. The Kurds had often rebelled against earlier Iraqi governments, receiving military support from Iran until 1975. The Kurds rebelled again during the Iran-Iraq War, and Saddam then moved to crush the revolt brutally. After Kurds in the northern Iraqi town of Halabja had surrendered to occupying Iranian troops, Saddam ordered a poison gas attack on the town. About 5,000 people were killed and 10,000 injured—the majority of the casualties were civilians, many of them children. This action forced thousands of Kurds to resettle in southern Iraq. Although Halabja was the largest single attack, many more chemical attacks followed on the Kurdish population in smaller villages.

annexing the country six days later. Saddam gained support from Yemen and Sudan, but the international community condemned Iraq, and a coalition formed to force Iraqi troops out of Kuwait.

The Gulf War of 1991

In February 1991, after Saddam had refused to withdraw troops from Kuwait, the military coalition, led by the United States, began a five-week bombing campaign of Iraqi

An Iraqi Kurd mourns her children who died during the 1988 Halabja attack. They were just two of 5,000 people who were killed by the poison gas attack.

The main bombing campaign of the US-led coalition began on March 21, 2003. Baghdad was subjected to heavy bombing, involving some 1,700 air attacks, in an operation known as "Shock and Awe."

positions in Kuwait. In the ground war that followed, up to 100,000 Iraqi troops were killed. The coalition called a cease-fire, and Iraq agreed to comply with United Nations Security Council resolutions, which included paying compensation to Kuwait and giving up its banned weapons of mass destruction (WMD).

Weapons inspections and sanctions

During the 1990s, suspected sites of WMD development were regularly inspected by UNSCOM (the United Nations Special Commission). Meanwhile, ordinary Iraqis suffered badly under the economic sanctions that were imposed on the country by the United Nations. In late 1998, the Iraqi government decided to refuse to cooperate with the weapons inspectors from UNSCOM until sanctions were lifted. President Bill Clinton, backed by Britain, retaliated with four days of air attacks. None of the subsequent 700 weapons inspections produced any evidence that Iraq was actively developing WMD.

Invasion of Iraq

Increasingly, the Iraqi regime came to be viewed by many Western countries, particularly the United States and the UK, as a threat to political stability in the region. Western governments condemned Iraq for its supposed possession of WMD and its defiance of UN resolutions. Iraq was also, according to the US administration, part of the "axis of evil" consisting of Iraq, Iran, and North Korea—states that supported terrorism.

In March 2003, a US-led coalition invaded Iraq. The coalition launched missile attacks on Iraqi targets, followed by a ground invasion. On April 9, after nearly three weeks of fighting, US troops took control of Baghdad. The overthrow of Saddam's regime was nearly complete.

Post-Saddam Iraq

In the days following the fall of Baghdad, coalition forces brought other major cities such as Kirkuk, Mosul, and Saddam's hometown of Tikrit under their control. On May 1, 2003, President George W. Bush declared that the war was over. Saddam and other key figures of the regime had gone into hiding.

The initial euphoria following Saddam's overthrow did not last long. Law and order broke down completely, and chaos reigned in many of the cities' streets. The coalition government had disbanded the Iraqi army, and coalition forces were unable to cope with the crisis as looting, bombings, and kidnappings occurred on a daily basis.

Trying to restore order to post-Saddam Iraq has been the major challenge for coalition troops since 2003. Coalition forces found themselves confronted by a powerful insurgency, including former members of the Baath regime, former Iraqi soldiers, and supporters of the radical Shia cleric Moqtada al-Sadr. In addition to Iraqi-born

On 9 April 2003, Iraqis demolished a statue of Saddam Hussein in the main square in Baghdad to celebrate the fall of the dictator. Using an American tank, US marines helped to topple the statue.

FOCUS: SADDAM FOUND GUILTY

In December 2003, Saddam Hussein was finally discovered in hiding near his native town of Tikrit. In October 2005, he went on trial before the Iraqi High Tribunal, charged with the murder of 148 Iraqis from the mainly Shia town of Dujail in 1982. The prosecutors chose to focus on this atrocity among the many that Saddam was responsible for because they believed it would be the easiest to compile evidence for and prosecute. Saddam was accused of crimes against humanity, including the torture of women and children and willful killing. In November 2006, Saddam was found guilty of the charges and sentenced to death by hanging. He was executed on December 30, 2006.

insurgents, they faced foreign Islamist volunteers, including those linked to the terrorist network Al Qaeda, who want to establish a Sunni caliphate in Iraq.

Originally, the controversial invasion of Iraq had been justified by the argument that Iraq possessed WMD. As time went on and no weapons of mass destruction were discovered in Iraq, the British and American administrations began to emphasize another reason for the invasion: the hope that

Iraq, without Saddam, could become a pro-Western democracy.

On the road to democracy?

In May 2003, the occupying forces established the Coalition Provisional Authority (CPA) as a transitional government for Iraq. Meanwhile, resistance to the coalition forces continued, and attacks intensified. The Shia holy city of Najaf and the Sunni stronghold of Fallujah were sites of particularly violent clashes. In 2004, the process for establishing a new Iraqi government began. The CPA transferred power to the Iraqi interim government in June 2004, and Iyad Allawi, a Shia, became interim prime minister.

Following the National Assembly election in January 2005, the Iraqi transitional government was installed. Iraq's first democratic elections saw 8 million Iraqis turn out to cast their votes, despite considerable intimidation by Sunni insurgents. Ibrahim al-Jaafari became prime minister, and Jalal Talabani, a Kurd, became the first non-Arab to be president of an Arab country.

In early 2007, as violence and insurgency continued to haunt the new Iraq, the US government decided to intensify its military presence in the major trouble spots of Baghdad and the province of al-Anbar by deploying an extra 30,000 US troops in these areas. By early 2008, the "surge," as this strategy was known, appeared to be relatively successful, significantly reducing the rate of violence and number of deaths.

An Iraqi insurgent takes aim. Many Iraqis agree with the main purpose of the insurgency, which is to rid Iraq of the US-led occupation.

CHAPTER 3

Social Changes

The ancient land of Mesopotamia, which spawned complex cultures such as the Sumerians, Akkadians, Babylonians, and Assyrians, has often been described as the cradle of civilization. Since this auspicious beginning, Iraq has had a long and difficult journey to the present day. Yet despite war and hardship, it remains a country with a rich, varied, and diverse culture.

Diversity of cultures

Iraq has one of the most multicultural populations in the Middle East. Ethnically, about 80 percent of its 27 million people are Arab, while

POPULATION

Population in Iraq today: 27,499,638

Ages

0–14 years: 39.4% (male 5,509,736; female 5,338,722)

15-64 years: 57.6% (male 8,018,841; female 7,812,611)

65 years and over: 3% (male 386,321; female 433,407)

Life expectancy

total population: 69 years

male: 68 years

female: 71 years

Ethnic groups

Arab: 75%–80%

Kurdish: 15%–20%

Turkmen, Assyrian, or other: 5%

Source: *CIA World Factbook*, 2007 (est.)

Population by religion

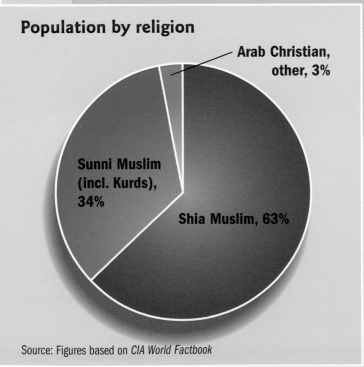

Arab Christian, other, 3%

Sunni Muslim (incl. Kurds), 34%

Shia Muslim, 63%

Source: Figures based on *CIA World Factbook*

approximately 4 million, or 15 percent of the total figure, are Kurdish. There are also much smaller but long-established pockets of Persians, Iraqi Turkmen, Assyrians, Chaldeans, and Yezidis. The Marsh Arabs trace their descent from the Sumerian and Babylonian cultures of ancient Mesopotamia.

As this chart shows, 97 percent of Iraq's population is Muslim. Shia Muslims outnumber Sunni Muslims (including the Kurds) by almost two to one.

Sunni Muslims worship during Friday prayers at Um al-Qura mosque in Baghdad. Most of Iraq's Arab Sunni Muslims live in Baghdad and in the valleys of the Euphrates and the Tigris, north of Baghdad.

Religion

Islam is the official religion of Iraq, and 97 percent of the population is Muslim. Ninety percent of the world's Muslims are Sunni, but unlike in most other Arab countries, Shias form the majority of Iraq's Muslims. (Neighboring non-Arab Iran also has a predominantly Shia population.) Iraq's Sunni Muslims, including the Kurds, are outnumbered by Shia Muslims by approximately two to one. There are some Arab Christian groups in Iraq, mainly Assyrians, but also some Orthodox Armenians.

The aftermath of the invasion

After the invasion of Iraq by US-led coalition forces and the demise of Saddam's Sunni-dominated regime in 2003, the Shia Muslims became the most influential ethnic group in Iraq, owing to their greater numbers. However, many Shias were unwilling to support the foreign occupation and were stirred to revolt. The Sunni Muslims had dominated the country under Saddam. They had the most to lose from the invasion, and many joined the post-invasion insurgency. The 4 million non-Arab Iraqi Kurds were relieved that their former persecutor, Saddam Hussein, had been deposed. They pressurized the new government to grant them a fully autonomous region in the north.

Ethnic conflict

In addition to fighting the occupation, many Sunnis and Shias also began fighting each other. Although Saddam's dictatorial regime was officially secular, it had favored the Sunni minority. Sunni Muslims tended to hold more positions of power, and Saddam had repressed the Shia majority and persecuted the Kurds. The Shias were bitter about the decades of oppression they had suffered at the hands of the Sunnis. With Saddam's removal, these grievances erupted into open conflict. The Sunnis, meanwhile, were angry at their loss of status and fearful of a Shia-dominated Iraq. Hundreds of Sunnis and Shias joined militias to fight their rivals.

Civil breakdown

With the disbandment of Iraqi police and army by the end of 2003 (later replaced by smaller forces), Iraqi citizens were threatened by indiscriminate violence, bombings, murders, and kidnappings. The infrastructure had also broken down, and electricity and water supplies had become disrupted.

As the violence worsened in 2005 and 2006, many streets in Baghdad became war zones.

There are up to 6 million Iraqi Kurds, mainly living in the northeast of the country. This small Kurdish farming village is typical of many situated in the foothills of Iraq's mountain ranges, separating the country from Turkey and Iran.

Armed neighborhood-watch groups manned barriers to protect their homes from death squads of rival ethnic groups. Meanwhile, ordinary Iraqis struggled to go on with their normal routines: going to school, obtaining food and getting to work.

Many Iraqis have died in the violence. According to a British-based research group, Iraq Body Count, over 90,000 civilians died in the five years after April 2003. Some put the number even higher. A survey carried out by a team of American and Iraqi physicians, published in the medical journal *Lancet*, estimated that between April 2003 and July 2006, 655,000 civilians died. This included deaths from disease caused by conditions arising from the conflict as well as violent deaths.

Shias

Arab Shia Muslims are based mainly in southern Iraq. The country's second-largest city, Basra, with a population of about 2 million, is predominantly Shia. As the country's major religious group, Shias desire greater recognition of their interests by the government. The two most influential figures in the Iraqi Shia community today are Ayatollah Ali al-Sistani and Moqtada al-Sadr. Al-Sistani is a man of moderate views, who wants to ease confrontation between coalition troops and the Shia community. However, radical Shia cleric Moqtada al-Sadr is determined to resist the foreign occupation. His Mahdi Army, a powerful paramilitary force, controls Shia areas in Baghdad, Basra, and other parts of southern Iraq. Since August 2007, the Mahdi Army has observed a cease-fire. Although al-Sadr refuses to disband his mass movement of mainly poor young Shias, there are signs that he is taking much more of a political role in Iraq.

Sunnis

There are over 5 million Arab Sunni Muslims, based mainly in central Iraq, making up approximately 20 percent of the Iraqi population. The Sunnis enjoyed a privileged status under Saddam, and of all the groups in Iraq, they had the most to lose from the 2003 invasion. Since Saddam's regime fell, many Sunni Muslims have felt dispossessed and excluded from the making of the new Iraq. Some, including former Baathists and members of the Iraqi military, have joined the insurgency. Initially, many of them aimed to restore Saddam's regime. Following his death, the broader aims of the Sunni insurgency have been to restore Sunni power in Iraq. However, there are disagreements among the many Sunni groups about what kind of regime they want to install. Islamists hope to establish Sharia (Islamic holy) law in Iraq, while nationalists aim to found a secular state.

Kurds

Based in the northeast of the country, Iraqi Kurds are mostly Sunni Muslims but consider themselves a separate people from Arab Muslims. Traditionally, Kurds led a simple, nomadic lifestyle, herding sheep and goats. They are a fiercely independent people who have waged a long struggle for autonomy within Iraq since the 1920s. In 1970, the Kurds achieved a measure of autonomy with the establishment of the Kurdistan Regional Government.

COMPARING COUNTRIES: POPULATION DENSITY

Iraq's population is mainly centered around its towns and cities. Iraq is less crowded than its neighbor Syria but has a higher population density than Iran.

Australia: less than 1 per sq mi (2 per sq km)

Iran: 16 per sq mi (42 per sq km)

Iraq: 24 per sq mi (62 per sq km)

Japan: 125 per sq mi (320 per sq km)

Saudi Arabia: 5 per sq mi (12 per sq km)

Syria: 36 per sq mi (93 per sq km)

United Kingdom: 90 per sq mi (231 per sq km)

United States: 10 per sq mi (25 per sq km)

Since then, the Iraqi government has frequently tried to reassert its control over the region. In the late 1980s, Saddam launched Operation Anfal, a series of attacks on the Kurds that caused the deaths of thousands, including those who perished in the infamous chemical attack on Halabja in 1988. In 1991, Iraqi Kurds rose up against the Saddam regime. Iraqi forces crushed the rebellion, killing hundreds and forcing thousands to flee to the Turkish border. The United States and the UK established no-fly zones in the 1990s to create a "safe haven" in northern Iraq for the Kurds.

CASE STUDY: KIRKUK

The northern city of Kirkuk contains a mixture of ethnic groups and cultures, including Assyrians, Kurds, Armenians, Arabs, and Iraqi Turkmen. The city is at the hub of the northern Iraqi oil industry. The Kurdistan Regional Government has de facto control over Kirkuk. It would like to make its control of the city official, but it is facing resistance from the non-Kurdish population, who claim the Kurds want the city only for its oil. A referendum to determine the future of the city is likely to be held in mid-2008.

The position of the Iraqi Kurds has improved considerably since 2003. Their semi-autonomous status has been officially recognized in the new federal Iraq. Many Kurds have been able to achieve relative prosperity since the region has been able to recover and develop more quickly than the rest of Iraq. Much of the wealth stems from the oil industry in northern Iraq.

Turkmen

The Turkish-speaking Turkmen are the third-largest ethnic group in Iraq after the Arabs and the Kurds. There are around 2 million

A firefighter helps put out a blaze after the bombing of an Assyrian church in Baghdad on August 1, 2004. Car bombs exploded outside several Christian churches in Iraq on the same day, killing at least 11 and injuring many more. These attacks were timed to coincide with Sunday evening prayers in the churches.

Turkmen, although they believe that their numbers are constantly underestimated in official statistics. The Turkmen are a mixture of Sunni and Shia Muslims as well as some Christians. In an attempt to disperse the Turkmen, Saddam Hussein forced them to move away from their homes, but many have returned to live in the north, around oil-rich Kirkuk.

Christians

Some 800,000 Christians were living in Iraq in 2003 (the figure today is not known for sure). The vast majority of these were Assyrians, chiefly descended from communities that did not convert to Islam in the seventh century CE. The Assyrian Christians are divided into sects, known as Chaldeans, Jacobites, and Nestorians. There are also some 20,000 Armenian Christians in the country.

Iraq's Christians were not persecuted by Saddam. In fact, his deputy prime minister was a Christian. Since 2003, however, the Christian minority has

Young Marsh Arabs harvest reeds in the eastern marshes of southern Iraq in July 2005. About 5,000 Iraqis have returned to reclaim land and restore the marshes after they had been drained by Saddam Hussein. Saddam had acted in retaliation for the Marsh Arabs' 1991 rebellion against his regime.

been targeted by both Sunni and Shia militias. Faced with violence, including beheadings and kidnappings, up to half of Iraq's Christians have now fled the country.

Marsh Arabs

The Marsh Arabs, also known as the Madan, had a unique and ancient culture in the marshlands of southern Iraq. They built reed boats and homes, fished, and herded water buffalo. Seminomadic, they were directly descended from the Sumerian and Babylonian cultures of ancient Mesopotamia. Other peoples tended to avoid the inhospitable marshland where they lived, allowing their unique culture and lifestyle to remain almost unchanged for over 5,000 years.

After the Gulf War of 1991, Marsh Arabs, along with the Kurds in northern Iraq, rose up in an unsuccessful rebellion against Saddam Hussein's government. Saddam's retaliation was to drain the marshland, causing the disintegration of Marsh Arab culture. They were forced to leave their homes, and many fled to refugee camps in Iran to the east. Plans to restore the marshlands appear to have had limited success. Once, this unique habitat was home to about 250,000 Marsh Arabs; today, it contains only a few thousand who have returned to the region.

Displaced Iraqis and refugees

Since 2003, one in six Iraqis have fled their homes. By early 2008, a total of 4.5 million Iraqis had been uprooted by the chaos and violence in the country. Of these, 2.5 million were displaced but still living within Iraq, and another 2 million had fled to neighboring countries such as Syria and Jordan. The majority of Iraqi refugees—about 1.5 million—went to Syria, but the country

Iraqi brothers get ready to attend their first day of school in Amman, Jordan. Their family fled the violence in Baqouba, north of Baghdad, in 2005. Two years later, the refugees were still looking for a permanent home.

struggled to provide the necessary food, shelter, and medical attention for such a large influx of people. In October 2007, Syria imposed entry restrictions on Iraqi refugees, permitting only merchants, businessmen, and university professors with visas to enter the country.

According to the United Nations High Commissioner for Refugees (UNHCR), some groups of Iraqi citizens were particularly vulnerable to attack by other Iraqis and needed to be moved far away from their hometowns and cities. These included Iraqis who had worked for the US-led administration in the early days of the occupation or, for example, with Western journalists and humanitarian agencies. Many Iraqis viewed these people as "collaborators." Wealthy Iraqis were in

CASE STUDY: GOING HOME

By the end of 2007, the Iraqi government was growing concerned about the drain on human resources, with so many people leaving the country. The government offered a cash and gift incentive for Iraqis to return to their homeland. According to the International Organization for Migration, returning families were each handed 1 million dinars (about $800) to assist them in their resettlement in Iraq. Many Iraqi families returned to find their former homes and businesses occupied by other displaced Iraqi families. The challenge for the Iraqi government is to find new houses for those people who they are encouraging to come home.

danger of being kidnapped, for ransoms as high as $60,000. Ethnic minorities, such as Christians or Palestinians, were also at high risk. In the four years from December 2003, 44 percent of Iraqis seeking asylum in Syria were Christians.

Resettlement and asylum

In September 2007, the United States promised to resettle 12,000 Iraqis and had accepted 2,600 by the end of that year. The UK accepted just 24 Iraqis for resettlement during 2007. The UNHCR stated that European Union countries could help more. Sweden has been the most generous, allowing a total of 90,000 Iraqis to settle in the country.

In addition to those Iraqis looking for resettlement through UNHCR, many applied for asylum in other countries. In 2007, 45,000 Iraqis applied for asylum, twice the number who applied in 2006. In March 2008, human rights groups criticized the British government for deporting hundreds of Iraqi asylum seekers back to central and southern Iraq. The following month, the British government announced plans to airlift up to 2,000 Iraqis to the UK. These included Iraqi translators who had helped the British army.

Iraqi refugees line up at an aid center in Damascus, Syria, in December 2007. They are waiting to receive food rations from aid workers for the United Nations High Commissioner for Refugees (UNHCR) and the World Food Program (WFP).

CHAPTER 4

★ Political Changes

There have been enormous political changes in the post-Saddam era, and in early 2008, Iraq's complex new political order was still in a state of development. After more than 20 years of totalitarian rule under Saddam Hussein, Iraq is now a parliamentary democracy, with every Iraqi citizen over the age of 18 able to vote. However, the government faces many difficult challenges, not least the task of restoring peace and security to the country. Deeply entrenched ethnic and religious divisions in Iraq make the task of forming a truly representative government especially difficult. Disagreements between representatives of the rival groups make it harder for the government to act decisively and can often cause the political process to become paralyzed.

FOCUS: THE JUDICIARY

The judiciary was often bypassed during the Saddam era, when a small ruling clique decided who was guilty and how they should be punished. The 2005 constitution established an independent judicial branch of government, consisting of two bodies:

- The Supreme Judicial Council manages and oversees the work of the country's law courts.
- The Supreme Court interprets the constitution, determines whether a law is constitutional, settles disputes between the federal government and the regions, and acts as a final court of appeal. The constitution's legal system is based on a mixture of European civil and Islamic law.

The Iraqi constitution

The chief task of the Iraqi transitional government (May 2005–May 2006) was to draft a permanent

Iraqi prime minister Nouri al-Maliki (right) receives President Jalal Talabani at his office in Baghdad on March 5, 2008.

During a special session of parliament, Iraqi MPs laid flowers on the seat of a member of the National Front for Iraqi Dialogue, a small Sunni party, who was killed in a suicide bombing on April 12, 2007.

constitution. Fifty-five members of parliament formed a special committee for the task, and the new constitution was narrowly approved by Iraqi voters on October 15, 2005. The constitution provides the framework for the new parliamentary democracy of Iraq. Because of Iraq's religious and ethnic divisions, the framers opted to create a federated state with a weak central government and strong regional administrations. The central government consists of three branches: the executive, the legislature, and the judiciary.

The executive branch is composed of a president as head of state and a prime minister as head of government. The president's position is chiefly ceremonial. Among other duties, he endorses treaties and laws, and following an election, he calls on the majority party to form a government. Political power rests with the prime minister and the cabinet. The cabinet is a group of senior officials appointed by the prime minister to advise on policy. Each member of the cabinet runs a department of state. Jalal Talabani, a Kurdish leader, was elected president of Iraq in April 2005. In December 2005, Ibrahim al-Jaafari, a Shia, became Iraq's prime minister following his party's victory in the parliamentary elections.

Al-Jaafari failed to win Kurdish and Sunni support in parliament, and in April 2006, President Talabani asked Nouri al-Maliki to succeed al-Jaafari as prime minister.

COMPARING COUNTRIES: POLITICAL SYSTEMS

US Government

The United States is a federal republic with a written constitution. Some powers are vested in the federal government, and other powers are assigned to the individual states that make up the federation. Its legislative branch, known as Congress, consists of the House of Representatives and the Senate. The executive branch consists of the president and the cabinet. The president is both head of state and head of government.

Iraqi Government

Iraq is a parliamentary democracy with a written constitution. Its legislative branch is the Council of Representatives (with the likely addition of a revising chamber, the Council of Unions, in the future). The executive branch consists of the prime minister, the president, and the cabinet. The prime minister is head of government. The president fulfills the ceremonial role of head of state and holds little political power.

An Iraqi woman shows her inked finger after voting in the constitutional referendum in Baghdad in October 2005. Iraqi voters turned out to approve a new constitution, which aimed to create an Islamic federal democracy.

The legislature, or lawmaking branch of government, consists of two assemblies—the Council of Representatives and the Council of Unions. The Council of Representatives has 275 members, elected by proportional representation. The Council of Unions does not yet exist. When it does, it is likely to take the form of an upper house, scrutinizing and revising the laws passed by the Council of Representatives. It will probably consist of representatives of Iraq's

18 governorates (local administrative divisions) and one autonomous region, the Kurdistan Regional Government.

Toward the first full-term government

After the invasion of Iraq, the coalition formed the Coalition Provisional Authority (CPA) to administer Iraq until an Iraqi government could be established. In June 2004, political power was officially transferred from the CPA to the Iraqi interim government, although the United States continued to a wield significant power behind the scenes. The interim government, headed by Iyad Allawi, served as a caretaker government until a representative government could be formed following elections. Elections were held for the Iraqi National Assembly in January 2005. In May, the interim government was replaced by the Iraqi transitional government, whose members were approved by the National Assembly. The transitional government drafted a new consititution for Iraq and made way, in May 2006, for Iraq's first full-term government.

Political parties

In a country with deep ethnic and religious divisions, political parties naturally evolved to represent these different groups and the subgroups within them. In the elections for the Council of Representatives in December 2005, the Unified Iraqi Alliance (UIA) won 128 out of the 275 seats. The UIA is a coalition of many groups but consists mainly of the two religious Shia groups—the Daawa (or "Call") Party and the Supreme Council of the Islamic Revolution in

FOCUS: POLITICAL COALITIONS

SHIAS
United Iraqi Alliance (coalition of many Shia groups, including the Daawa Party, the Supreme Council of the Islamic Revolution in Iraq, and Moqtada al-Sadr's party)

SUNNIS
Iraqi Accord Front (coalition of three Sunni groups: the Iraqi Islamic Party, the General Council for the People of Iraq, and the Iraqi National Dialogue Council)

KURDS
Kurdistan Alliance (coalition of many Kurdish groups, including the Patriotic Union of Kurdistan and the Kurdistan Democratic Party)

SECULAR
Iraqi National List (a secular alliance of Shias and Sunnis)

CASE STUDY: THE KURDISH AUTONOMOUS REGION

The success of the Kurdistan Alliance in the January 2005 elections gave the Kurds a strong position in the Iraqi Transitional Government and allowed them to reassert their special status within Iraq. Under the 2005 constitution, the Kurdistan Regional Government (KRG) became the official government of the region, with control over all domestic affairs. The federal government kept control of foreign affairs and coalition forces retained control of security. In May 2007, the KRG took over responsibility for security. By early 2008, many Iraqis were growing resentful of the Kurds' elevated position within Iraqi politics. They were concerned about the Kurdish region becoming too powerful and possibly seceding (becoming completely independent) from Iraq. Many feared that the Kurds would take control of the profitable oil fields in that part of the country.

Iraq. The al-Sadr bloc, led by radical Shia cleric Moqtada al-Sadr and backed by the Sadrist Movement, won 32 seats.

Ten seats short of an overall majority, the UIA formed a coalition government with the Kurdistan Alliance, which, with 53 seats, was the second-highest bloc. The Kurdistan Alliance is also a coalition of many groups, the most significant of which are the Patriotic Union of Kurdistan (PUK) and the Kurdistan Democratic Party (KDP).

The Iraqi National List, headed by former prime minister Iyad Allawi, is a secular alliance of Shias and Sunnis. It performed badly in the elections, gaining just 25 seats in parliament. The Iraqi Accord Front consists of three Sunni parties: the Iraqi Islamic Party, the General Council for the People of Iraq, and the Iraqi National Dialogue Council.

CHAPTER 5

Economic Changes

Iraq has a mostly state-owned economy, meaning that much of its industry is owned and run by the government. It is an oil-rich country, and since the 1920s, its economy has been heavily dependent on oil production along with the related industries of oil refining and chemical and fertilizer manufacture.

Iraq's economy has been severely damaged by the chaos and disorder since 2003. In 2007, up to a third of the workforce was unemployed. Iraq has great economic potential, however. It possesses a wealth of resources, including oil, natural gas, phosphates, and sulfur. Construction is another major growth area with so much rebuilding necessary as a result of the war and insurgency.

Oil

Iraq has proven reserves of 115 billion barrels of oil. The major reserves are based in Kirkuk in the north and Rumaila in the south. However, Iraq's

Iraq has proven reserves of 115 billion barrels of oil, the fourth-largest reserves in the world. However, Iraq's oil infrastructure is in urgent need of investment.

statistics have not been revised since 2001 and it is likely that the country possesses another 50 to 100 billion barrels of recoverable oil.

Huge quantities of oil were discovered near Kirkuk in 1927, but it was not until the 1970s that then vice president Saddam Hussein began to exploit Iraq's massive oil wealth to transform the country. Saddam used oil revenues to build new factories, roads, and railways and set up better health care and education facilities. By 1979, oil represented 95 percent of the country's export earnings and

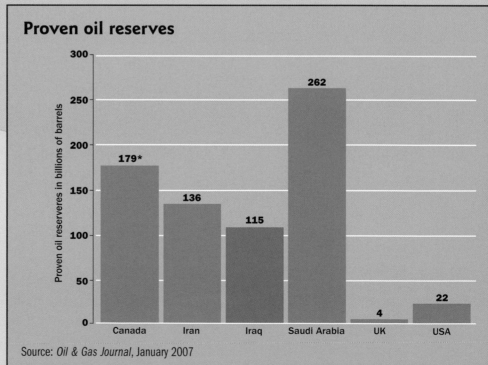

Proven oil reserves

Proven oil reserves in billions of barrels

- Canada: 179*
- Iran: 136
- Iraq: 115
- Saudi Arabia: 262
- UK: 4
- USA: 22

Source: *Oil & Gas Journal*, January 2007

*The majority of Canada's 179 billion barrels consists of oil sand reserves, not conventional crude oil reserves.

A gas tanker blazes after an insurgent attack in Baghdad. Terrorists and foreign fighters have targeted Iraq's oil industry since the occupation, also sabotaging oil pipelines and installations.

Iraq was the second-largest exporter of oil in the world after Saudi Arabia. Oil production peaked at 3.5 million barrels of oil per day (mbd) in July 1990.

By 1980, Iraq had the second-largest economy in the Arab world after Saudi Arabia. However, during the 1980s, the economy was badly hit by the war with Iran, which caused economic losses of approximately $100 billion. International sanctions during the 1990s dealt an additional blow. Oil production practically ceased during the 2003 invasion. Since then, production has been severely disrupted because of attacks on the oil industry infrastructure by insurgents.

Despite this, crude oil exports grew steadily during 2007 to reach prewar levels in November. By February 2008, total oil production averaged 2.4 mbd, of which exports accounted for 1.93 mbd. Iraq's oil refineries are in drastic need of investment and modernization, however. In 2007,

Iraq was importing about a third of its diesel and kerosene and over half of its gasoline. With better refineries, all of these products could be made from Iraqi oil.

Another problem facing the oil industry was oil smuggling. According to an April 2008 parliamentary committee report, an estimated $5 billion (or approximately 10 percent of total oil revenues) was being lost each year due to smuggling.

The distribution of oil revenues remains a contentious issue. In April 2008, the Iraqi government discussed reestablishing the Iraqi National Oil Company as a way of regulating the oil industry and sharing oil revenues more fairly between Sunni, Shia, and Kurd regions.

Iraq's economy has been struggling for many years. The United Nations imposed sanctions on Iraq after its 1990 invasion of Kuwait, preventing Iraq from exporting any of its produce. Although oil was its largest export, a wide range of other products were also affected, including dates, cotton, and fertilizers. Iraq's economy began to recover after 1995 with the oil-for-food program. This program, supervised by the UN, allowed Iraq to export oil in exchange for food, medicine, and other essential goods.

Following the 2003 invasion, both the sanctions and the oil-for-food program were ended. Nevertheless, Iraq continues to be burdened by a huge foreign debt, due in part to its high military expenditures under Saddam.

Children stack freshly made bricks to dry in the sun at a brick factory in the southern Iraqi town of Samawa. Children as young as seven labor alongside adult workers to produce up to 100,000 bricks each month to meet the high demand for rebuilding in Basra and other towns in southern Iraq.

Natural resources

In addition to oil, Iraq possesses enormous proven natural gas resources in the north and south of the country. This resource remains largely untapped due to poorly maintained gas-processing facilities and a lack of investment in the industry.

Iraq has abundant mineral deposits, including phosphates (used to make fertilizers) and sulfur.

Experts believe that its mineral reserves are among the largest in the world.

Iraq also possesses construction materials such as steel, stone, and gypsum (for cement manufacture), which will be useful for the rebuilding of Iraq's battered cities. In November 2007, the Iraqi government pledged $1.8 billion for reconstruction in Baghdad.

Power

Iraq obtains its energy from a mixture of sources, including oil, natural gas, and hydropower. All of its power-generating plants are in need of investment and rebuilding after suffering heavy damage from coalition attacks in the 1991 Gulf War and the 2003 invasion and sabotage by insurgents since then. Because of the damage power plants have suffered, power supplies in most towns and cities continue to be intermittent

FOCUS: COMMUNICATIONS

Iraq's telecommunications system was badly damaged during the 2003 invasion, and the network's coverage remains poor. For every 100 residents, there are approximately five main telephone lines and ten television sets. However, this has not prevented Iraqis from communicating. An estimated 11 million Iraqis use mobile phones and Internet access is growing. Perhaps the world's most famous 'blog' was posted by an Iraqi, known as Salam Pax or the Baghdad Blogger, recording his comments on everyday life and the war in Iraq.

and irregular. For example, in 2007, the electricity supply to Baghdad averaged just eight hours per day.

Agriculture and forestry

Until the 1950s, Iraq's economy was mostly based on agriculture. Arable land now makes up just 13 percent of Iraq's total land. About half of this land is irrigated in order to make it productive. Iraq's major agricultural products are fruit, vegetables, and grain crops such as wheat and barley. Other crops include rice, millet, maize, dates, sugarcane, and cotton. The northern Kurdish regions are known especially for their livestock products, including milk, wool, and hides. In recent decades, many of Iraq's forested areas have been chopped down for timber and paper products. Today, trees cover less than 2 percent of the country's land area and most wood is imported.

Gross domestic product (GDP) is an economic measure to show the value of all goods and services produced in a country in one year. The chart divides this into sectors: agriculture, industry, and services. In comparison, the United States' largest sector is services (78 percent), followed by industry (21 percent) and agriculture (just 1 percent).

GDP composition by sector

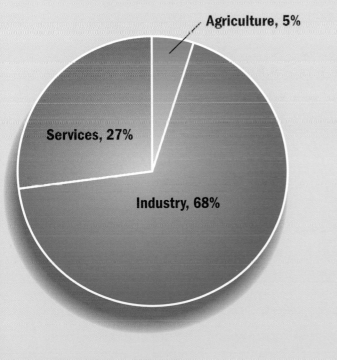

Agriculture, 5%

Services, 27%

Industry, 68%

Source: *CIA World Factbook*, 2006 (est.)

CHAPTER 6

Changing Relationships

Today's Iraq has been shaped to a great extent by recent relationships with other countries and organizations. Iraq's present relationships with the United States, the European Union, the United Nations, and its neighbors in the Middle East, particularly Iran, are also likely to play a large part in determining its future.

The United States

Since 2003, when it led the invasion to topple the Saddam regime, the United States has been the dominant external influence on Iraq. In fact, US influence on Iraq had been growing steadily since

1982. From this time, the United States and other Western countries supported Iraq during its war with Iran (1980–88). When Saddam invaded neighboring oil-rich Kuwait in August 1990, US policy toward Iraq abruptly changed from one of support to outright hostility. In 1991, a US-led coalition expelled Iraqi forces from Kuwait. The US government then urged the Iraqi people to rise up against the dictator. When these uprisings failed, Saddam launched a brutal retaliation. The United States (with help from the UK) policed no-fly zones in northern and southern Iraq where Iraqi planes were forbidden to fly. This helped protect Kurds and Shias from Saddam.

The decision to invade

The Bush administration built a case for war against Iraq based on Saddam's suspected development of WMD, his flouting of UN resolutions, repeated obstruction of weapons inspectors, and suspected links with Al Qaeda as well as his brutal actions against his own people. The US government believed these constituted sufficient grounds for bringing about "regime change." According to the war's many critics, the primary reason for the war was actually to gain control of Iraqi oil. The decision to invade Iraq was particularly controversial because it was taken without explicit UN authorization.

FOCUS: "AXIS OF EVIL"

Iraq's relationship with the United States steadily deteriorated during the 2000s as Iraq refused to cooperate with weapons inspectors and flouted UN resolutions. In January 2002, President George W. Bush described Iraq, Iran, and North Korea collectively as an "axis of evil." President Bush believed that these countries supported terrorism against the United States and were intent on developing weapons of mass destruction. In the buildup to war in 2003, the Bush administration claimed that there were links between the Saddam regime and Al Qaeda, the terrorist network responsible for the 9/11 attacks. However, intelligence reports in 2006 concluded that there was no evidence of ties between Saddam and Al Qaeda.

Coalition troops are often vulnerable to attack. A US soldier stands guard near the Baghdad Hotel, scene of a recent explosion. Over 4,000 US troops have been killed in Iraq since the occupation.

US power in Iraq

In the immediate aftermath of Saddam's overthrow, many people hoped that the UN would oversee the establishment of a new Iraqi government. However, from April 2003 to June 2004, Iraq was effectively governed by the United States through the Coalition Provisional Authority (CPA), which assumed executive, legislative, and judicial authority over the country. The transfer of authority to an Iraqi government was made more difficult by the CPA policy of "de-Baathification." This policy entailed the removal of Baath Party members from their positions in the government and military, depriving the country of some of its most capable administrators.

The United States continued to wield power and influence following the transition to the Iraqi interim government in June 2004. At this time, the Americans strongly encouraged the rebuilding of Iraq's security forces and the return of Baathists to public service. The United States also gradually persuaded Sunni Arab representatives to enter the political process, and by May 2005, nearly a thousand Sunnis met in Baghdad to demand their inclusion in the drafting of the new constitution. The United States has wielded influence in a number of areas, helping to shape the Iraqi government's policies on the oil industry, its dealings with Iran, and the awarding of construction contracts.

United Nations Special Commission (UNSCOM) inspectors measure the volume of nerve gas in an Iraqi container after the Gulf War in 1991.

The US presence in Iraq

The US military presence in Iraq has been very costly in terms of human lives. In March 2008, the total number of US soldiers killed in Iraq had reached 4,000. It has also cost the US taxpayer a staggering amount. Two senior economists, Joseph Stiglitz and Linda Bilmes, claimed in 2008 that the financial cost of the war to the United States was between $1 trillion and $3 trillion. The higher figure included the cost of lifetime medical care for 65,000 injured US troops.

The war has also damaged the United States' standing in the Middle East, where it is perceived by many as an occupying power. The 2007 "surge" in troop numbers has improved the military situation and reduced the level of violence in the country, but this suggests that the country can only be pacified by a large and long-term US military presence. The United States faces a difficult dilemma. Many would like the troops to leave as soon as possible. Others argue that a hasty withdrawal would cause even greater disorder, possibly outright civil war, and destroy all the gains achieved since 2003. In 2006, the US

Congress authorized $1 billion to build several long-term military bases in Iraq. It seems likely that an American military presence in Iraq will continue for some time to come.

The United Nations

Under Saddam, Iraq was frequently criticized and condemned by the UN. Just days after Saddam's ill-fated attempt to annex Kuwait in August 1990, the United Nations Security Council imposed

CASUALTIES OF WAR

Number of deaths suffered by the forces of each coalition country in Iraq between March 2003 and March 2008:

United States: 4,000
United Kingdom: 175
Italy: 33
Poland: 23
Ukraine: 18
Bulgaria: 13
Spain: 11
Others: 35

Source: Iraq Coalition Casualty Count

comprehensive economic sanctions on Iraq, preventing it from trading. Saddam was not overthrown during the war, so the UN adopted a policy of containment. That is to say, they hoped to use measures such as economic sanctions to prevent or dissuade him from attempting further aggressive acts against foreign countries or his own people. Sanctions remained in place at the end of the war.

During the Iran-Iraq War and again against the Kurds, Saddam had used chemical weapons. He had also tried to develop nuclear weapons at a secret base at Osirak, near Baghdad, from the late 1970s, although this project was crippled by an Israeli surprise attack in 1981. Based on this evidence, the international community feared that Saddam was stockpiling weapons of mass destruction (WMD). In April 1991, the UN Security Council passed Resolution 687, which insisted that Iraq give "full, final, and complete disclosure" of its WMD and missiles to UNSCOM (the United Nations Special Commission). However, Saddam did not cooperate with UNSCOM. Although the sanctions caused great

suffering to the Iraqi people, they did not apply sufficient pressure on Saddam to make him cooperate with UN demands.

UN oil-for-food program

In 1995, the United Nations modified the sanctions regime to try to alleviate the suffering of ordinary Iraqis. It introduced the oil-for-food program, allowing Iraq to sell its oil in order to provide its people with the basic humanitarian needs of food and medicine. However, the program was controversial since much of the money was not spent on ordinary Iraqis. It also suffered from allegations of corruption, with some of its profits diverted to the Iraqi government and UN officials.

Saddam and the UN weapons inspectors

In October 1997, after encountering repeated noncooperation and obstruction during inspections of suspected WMD sites, UNSCOM reported to the UN Security Council that Iraq was in breach of Resolution 687. In 1998, to try to force Saddam to cooperate, US and British air forces launched a four-day bombing campaign on Iraq known as Operation Desert Fox. However, Iraq persisted in its refusal to readmit weapons inspectors.

In 2002, this warehouse in al-Taji, near Baghdad, was used, according to Iraqi authorities, to store food imported through the UN oil-for-food program. The authorities denied that it was used as a biological weapons facility, as the United States claimed.

In November 2002, the UN Security Council passed Resolution 1441, which again required Iraq to list all its WMD and give weapons inspectors the freedom to search wherever they wanted. The United States and UK favored war if Iraq did not comply but failed to get agreement on this with all the other UN Security Council members. When the invasion took place in March 2003, it was without explicit UN authorization.

Role of the UN today

The sanctions regime and the oil-for-food program ended with Saddam's overthrow in 2003. In 2004, a UN resolution transferred power to Iraq's elected rulers. The United Nations Security Council had not endorsed the invasion of Iraq, and its role in Iraq was minimal in the years following 2003. However, since the coalition and Iraqi forces have been unable to establish widespread peace and security in Iraq, UN

CASE STUDY: UN HEADQUARTERS BOMBED

On August 19, 2003, a truck bomb exploded outside the United Nations' headquarters in Baghdad. The explosion injured about a hundred people and killed 22, including the top UN envoy for Iraq, Sergio Vieira de Mello, a veteran of peacekeeping operations. The UN office in Baghdad had not been protected by coalition forces, and the bombing was one of the worst attacks in UN history. No group claimed responsibility for the attack. Following a second bomb attack on the UN office in September 2003, the United Nations effectively withdrew from Iraq, only returning in August 2007.

involvement is likely to increase. In August 2007, the UN Security Council voted to expand the role of the United Nations in Iraq.

Early in 2007, a US military spokesman alleged that weapons and bomb components like these were being made in Iran and smuggled to Iraqi Shia groups for use on US and Iraqi forces.

Young supporters of radical Shia cleric Moqtada al-Sadr march in the Shia-dominated Sadr City district of Baghdad. Al-Sadr has strong links with Iran, from which he has received funds and weapons for his powerful Mahdi Army. It is generally thought that al-Sadr is currently living in Iran.

Today, the focus of the United Nations is humanitarian. In February 2008, the organization appealed to member states for $265 million for food relief, clean water, medical supplies, and shelter for the Iraqi people. The United Nations also pledged to support the Iraqi authorities in offering aid to returning refugees and internally displaced persons (IDPs) and emphasized the need for improved access and security for aid workers in Iraq.

Iran

Iran and Iraq have had a long history of distrust and conflict, stretching back many centuries. In 1980, Saddam's Iraq invaded Iran. This was partly because of a border dispute but more significantly because Saddam feared that the Shia revolution in Iran, led by the charismatic cleric Ayatollah Khomeini, would inspire Iraq's Shias to rise up against Saddam's Sunni-dominated government. The ensuing eight-year conflict left up to 1 million Iranian and Iraqi people dead.

Tensions between the two countries have persisted since the end of the Iran-Iraq War. Iran's stance during the US-led invasion of Iraq in 2003 was one of "active neutrality." This meant that although Iran supported the invasion of Iraq to oust Saddam, it was unwilling to become involved in the conflict.

In 2006, US military commander General George Casey accused Iran of providing covert support to the Shia insurgency in Iraq. He accused Iran

of funding, training, and arming Shia militias to carry out bomb attacks on coalition forces and Iraqis. Iran denied the allegations of links with Shia militia groups, but Sunni Iraqis, in particular, are suspicious of Iranian intentions in Iraq. Some commentators believe that Iran wants to keep US forces bogged down in Iraq so they won't attack Iran. Others think that Iran is building up a resistance network in Iraq to hit back at US troops in the event of a US attack on Iran's nuclear facilities.

Iraqi refugees in the Syrian capital Damascus celebrate Iraq's 1–0 victory against Saudi Arabia to win the 2007 Asian Cup. Syria is host to some 1.5 million Iraqi refugees, most of whom live in Damascus.

A new spirit of cooperation has recently emerged between the two neighboring countries. In March 2008, Iranian president Mahmoud Ahmadinejad became the first Middle Eastern head of state to visit Iraq since the 2003 invasion. Ahmadinejad stressed that the two countries were now like brotherly neighbors and that the United States had no place in Iraq. He pledged $1 billion in loans and promised to supply the Iraqi national grid with electricity from power stations in Iran.

Syria

Relations between Iraq and its western neighbor Syria were terminated in 1982 when Syria sided with Iran in the Iran-Iraq War. Saddam saw this as a betrayal by his former friend and fellow Baathist, Syrian president Hafez al-Assad. In 1991, Syria formed part of the coalition to drive Iraq out of Kuwait.

In the post-Saddam era, relations between the two countries improved significantly. In November 2006, Syrian foreign minister Walid Muallim paid a historic visit to his Iraqi counterpart Hoshyar

Zebari in Baghdad to announce the restoration of all diplomatic ties between the two countries. The talks stressed the importance of cooperation between Iraq and Syria to achieve security and stability in the region.

For Iraq, a powerful incentive for restoring links with Syria was internal security. Since 2003, hundreds of foreign fighters, including Al Qaeda terrorists and suicide bombers, had crossed the Syria-Iraq border to join the Iraqi insurgency. With diplomatic relations restored, Syria pledged to do all it could to prevent any further unauthorized flow of people or weapons across the border.

Syria has a strong interest in helping to restore order and stability in Iraq to end the flood of refugees across its border. Between 2003 and 2007, some 1.5 million Iraqi refugees entered Syria. The country struggled to deal with such huge numbers and began to restrict access toward the end of 2007.

FOCUS: EUROPEAN UNION

From 1979 to 2003, the European Union (EU) had no political relations with Iraq. Since 2003, the EU has tried to help in the development of a secure, stable, and democratic Iraq. The EU is the second-largest exporter to Iraq (after Turkey), and a number of EU member states provide humanitarian relief. The European Commission has contributed nearly $1.3 billion toward the reconstruction of Iraq, and the EU will continue to play a significant part in improving living conditions for Iraq's citizens.

Turkey

Iraq's northern neighbor Turkey wants to see Iraq emerge from its present unstable position into a unified and prosperous nation. Trade is important between the countries, and the Turkish economy suffered greatly when the UN imposed economic sanctions on Iraq in the 1990s and early 2000s. Since then, the situation has improved. Iraq imported $3 billion of goods from Turkey in 2006.

However, the status of the northern Iraqi Kurds remains a source of tension between the two countries. The Turkish government fears that if the Iraqi Kurds gain complete autonomy, Kurds in Turkey will want independence too. In February 2008, Turkish troops crossed the border into northern Iraq in an operation to oust separatist PKK (Kurdistan Workers' Party) rebel bases. After a warning from the US government, Turkish troops quickly withdrew. Iraqi president Jalal Talabani visited Turkey in March 2008, and relations between the two countries appeared to be improving. It is likely, however, that Turkey's deep-seated insecurity about the Kurdish situation will persist.

Militants from the PKK (Kurdistan Workers' Party) listen to instructions from their team commander during a training session in a camp near Arbil in northern Iraq. The PKK are fighting Turkey for Kurdish self-rule in southeastern Turkey. Their use of northern Iraq as a safe haven from Turkish forces has been a source of tension between Turkey and Iraq since the PKK campaign began in 1984.

CHAPTER 7

Future Challenges

The main challenge facing Iraq is to restore peace, stability, and the rule of law. To do this, the government will need to find ways of appealing to the many armed and violent groups operating throughout the country and demonstrate to these groups that they can achieve at least some of their aims through the democratic political process. The government will need to encourage people to go beyond their ethnic and religious differences and think of themselves as fellow citizens of Iraq.

To many Iraqis, the occupation by US-led coalition troops is the main problem. Sunni Muslims, once the powerful elite under Saddam Hussein, Arab nationalists, and foreign fighters particularly resent and seek to resist the presence of Western troops in Iraq. However, many other Iraqis recognize the need for the continued presence of coalition forces. The newly formed Iraqi army and security forces are not yet able to maintain order by themselves, and a sudden withdrawal of coalition troops could cause Iraq to spiral down into civil war. Others see the US-led occupation as the main driving force behind the insurgency. In essence, the coalition forces are seen both as part of the problem and part of the solution.

Environmental issues

Iraq has a number of pressing environmental

POLL FOR UNITY

In 2008, Iraqis were asked in a poll about the future of Iraq. Do Iraqis want a unified Iraq?

95% of Sunnis said yes

67% of Shias said yes

10% of Kurds said yes

Poll conducted by D3 Systems for BBC News, ABC News, and others

concerns, including inadequate supplies of drinking water, a lack of decent sewerage systems, soil degradation (due to salination), and desertification. Iraq also suffers from pollution caused by oil spillages due to acts of sabotage on pipelines and leakages from aging oil wells. Chemical spills, depleted uranium (for example, from weapons and shells used in recent conflicts), and other hazardous substances pollute groundwater. The cleanup of some of Iraq's worst toxic "hot spots" began in early 2006. However, a lack of security and funds has hampered the operation's progress.

Where next?

The fragile new democracy in Iraq is struggling to assert itself against a backdrop of an unpopular foreign occupation and daily acts of violence and insurgency. If the government fails to achieve peace between the warring factions, Sunni and Shia divisions could worsen and spill over into the greater Middle East. Iran may exploit its close ties with the Iraqi Shias in order to extend its influence over Iraq. Turkey could threaten additional border incursions if it suspects Kurdish terrorists are seeking refuge in northern Iraq. And Iraq's refugees are a potential destabilizing factor in the region as a whole.

However, there are also some grounds for hope. In January 2005, 8.4 million Iraqis risked their lives in turning out to vote in the country's first general election since the invasion. In 2007, Sunni tribal leaders cooperated with Iraqi security forces to drive the terrorist group

Al Qaeda in Iraq out of Baghdad and the western province of Anbar. Small-scale events such as these suggest that many Iraqis want a stable and prosperous future for their country.

Sunni and Shia Muslims gather for Friday prayers as a sign of unity in the Abu Hanifa mosque in Adhamiya, Baghdad. Sunnis and Shias have lived for centuries in mixed neighborhoods, and there are also many religiously mixed families. Scenes like this one offer hope for a brighter future in Iraq.

Timeline

1920 League of Nations hands mandate to Great Britain to rule Iraq.

1921 Faisal I becomes king of Iraq.

1927 Significant quantities of oil are discovered in Iraq.

1932 Iraq becomes independent.

1958 The monarchy is overthrown by General Kassem's military coup. King Faisal II is killed.

1963 Kassem is overthrown by Colonel Arif's Baathist coup.

1968 President al-Bakr comes to power.

1969 Saddam Hussein becomes vice president.

1979 Saddam Hussein becomes president.

1980 Iran-Iraq War begins.

1988 Saddam uses chemical weapons to attack Kurds in Halabja.
Iran-Iraq War ends.

1990–91 Iraq invades Kuwait. Gulf War begins. UN imposes sanctions on Iraq.

Apr. 1995 UN oil-for-food program begins.

Dec. 1998 Iraq refuses to cooperate with UN weapons inspectors.

Jan. 2002 George W. Bush's "axis of evil" speech. United States demands "regime change" in Iraq.

Nov. 2002 UN passes Resolution 1441 (calling on Iraq to list all its WMD).

Mar. 2003 A US-led coalition invades Iraq.

Apr. 2003 Baghdad is captured.

May 2003 Coalition Provisional Authority (CPA) is established.

Jun. 2004 Iraqi interim government is set up.

Jan. 2005 Iraq holds first free elections for the newly set up National Assembly.

Apr. 2005 President Jalal Talabani is elected.

Jun. 2005 Kurdish parliament has its first session.

Oct. 2005 Saddam Hussein goes on trial. Constitution is approved by Iraqi voters.

Dec. 2005 Iraq holds parliamentary elections for Council of Representatives.

Apr. 2006 Nouri al-Maliki is named as Iraq's new prime minister.

Nov. 2006 Saddam Hussein is found guilty of "wilfull killing" and other charges.
Syrian and Iraqi foreign ministers meet.

Dec. 2006 Saddam Hussein is executed.

2007 "Surge" of extra US troops is deployed.

Sept. 2007 US Senate passes nonbinding resolution to divide Iraq into three regions as part of a federation.

Nov. 2007 Cash incentive offered to Iraqi refugees to return home.

Feb. 2008 Turkish troops cross Iraqi border, then withdraw after US warning.

Mar. 2008 President Jalal Talabani visits Turkey. Iran's president Mahmoud Ahmadinejad visits Iraq.

Glossary

Anfal A campaign waged by Saddam Hussein in 1988 against the Kurds.

arable Land that is suitable for growing crops.

asylum seeker A person looking for shelter or refuge in another country.

autonomous Having a large degree of self-government, or independence.

caliph The title of the successors of Mohammed as leaders of the Islamic world.

coalition A union of different groups or parties that come together for a common purpose, for example, to form a military force or a government.

collaborator A person who cooperates with others but may be seen as a traitor.

constitution A statement containing the basic laws by which a state is governed.

cuneiform A form of writing using wedge-shaped characters.

democracy A political system in which the people elect their own leaders.

federate Unite in a federal union.

federation The political unit formed by the union of several regions or states.

guerrilla A member of an irregular force waging war against larger, regular armed forces.

humanitarian Showing concern for others or to do with human rights.

infrastructure The structural elements of a country,

including its roads, airports, hospitals, and public utilities.

insurgency A rebellion or uprising, for example, against a government.

irrigate Supply land with water, using artificial canals and ditches.

Kurdish Autonomous Region A large administrative region in northern Iraq, originally formed in 1974. It gained autonomy with the help of coalition forces after the Gulf War.

Kurdistan "Land of the Kurds," a region situated to the north of Iraq but also part of neighboring Iran, Turkey, Syria, and Armenia.

mandate An assignment or official duty (for example, to command another territory).

militia A body of unofficial soldiers.

nomad A member of a tribe who moves from place to place to find food and pasture.

Ottoman empire A Turkish empire established in the late 13th century in Asia Minor, eventually extending through the Middle East. It came to an end in 1918.

parliamentary Relating to parliament, a nation's legislative body.

refugee A person who seeks refuge, especially from war or persecution, by going to a foreign country.

sanctions The special penalties or restrictions laid down by an organization as a punishment.

secular Nonreligious.

terrorism The deliberate use or threat of violence against civilian targets in pursuit of a political aim.

totalitarian rule Control by a dictator.

United Nations (UN) An international organization set up in 1945 to promote peace, security, and international cooperation.

weapons of mass destruction (WMD) Weapons that can kill large numbers of people and/or cause great damage to man-made structures and the environment. They include nuclear, chemical, and biological weapons.

Further information

Books

Allawi, Ali A. *The Occupation of Iraq: Winning the War, Losing the Peace.* Yale University Press, 2008.

King, John. *Iraq: Then and Now.* Raintree, 2005.

Pax, Salam. *The Baghdad Blog.* McArthur, 2003.

Tripp, Charles. *A History of Iraq.* Cambridge University Press, 2007.

DVD

Iraq in Fragments. Dir. James Longley. Drakes Avenue Pictures, 2007.
A three-part documentary about everyday life in Iraq seen through the eyes of one Sunni, one Shia and one Kurd.

Websites

iraq.usembassy.gov/
Website of the US embassy in Iraq, includes press releases.

news.bbc.co.uk/1/hi/world/middle_east/country_profiles/791014.stm
This BBC News site gives a profile of Iraq.

https://www.cia.gov/library/publications/the-world-factbook/geos/iz.html
Facts and figures about Iraq from the CIA.

www.economist.com/countries/Iraq/
A profile of Iraq and its economy.

www.historycentral.com/NationbyNation/Iraq/index.html
Information about all aspects of Iraq, including its government, geography, history, and people.

www.un.org/english
In the United Nations website, click on link "Situation in Iraq."

www.who.int/countries/irq/en/
Information about health in Iraq.

Index

Page numbers in **bold** refer to illustrations and charts.